THE PEACEFUL PENCIL

COLOURING MANDALAS

75 MINDFUL PATTERNS TO ENJOY

PEONY PRESS

RELAX AND UNWIND WITH THIS STRESS-RELIEVING COLOURING BOOK OF MEDITATIVE MANDALAS. THE ART OF COLOURING IS A FORM OF MEDITATION, FOCUSING THE MIND AND STILLING THE ENDLESS MENTAL CHATTER THAT SAPS OUR ENERGY AND CAUSES STRESS AND NEGATIVE FEELINGS. AS YOU START TO COLOUR IN THESE BEAUTIFUL MANDALAS YOU WILL UNLEASH YOUR INNER CREATIVITY AND FIND YOURSELF GRADUALLY MOVING TO A MORE PEACEFUL AND CALMING STATE OF MIND.

YOU CAN COLOUR IN AS LITTLE OR AS MUCH AS YOU LIKE, TAKING YOUR TIME TO DEVELOP YOUR PICTURE THE WAY YOU WANT IT. THERE ARE NO HARD AND FAST RULES, YOU ARE TRULY FREE TO CREATE YOUR OWN UNIQUE DESIGNS WHETHER YOU CHOOSE PENCILS, PENS OR PAINTS. START COLOURING TODAY AND ENJOY THE STILL, QUIET VOICE OF CALM THIS SIMPLE MEDITATIVE PRACTICE WILL BRING YOU.

IF YOU WANT TO CONQUER THE ANXIETY OF LIFE,
LIVE IN THE MOMENT, LIVE IN THE BREATH.

AMIT RAY

In the end, just three things matter:
How well we have lived, How well we have
loved, How well we have learned to let go.

Jack Kornfield

TO LIVE A CREATIVE LIFE, WE MUST LOSE
OUR FEAR OF BEING WRONG.

JOSEPH CHILTON PEARCE

WHAT WE ARE TODAY COMES FROM OUR
THOUGHTS OF YESTERDAY, AND OUR PRESENT
THOUGHTS BUILD OUR LIFE OF TOMORROW:
OUR LIFE IS THE CREATION OF OUR MIND.

BUDDHA

Life is available only in the present
moment. If you abandon the present moment
you cannot live the moments of your
daily life deeply.

Thich Nhat Hanh

EACH PERSON DESERVES A DAY AWAY
IN WHICH NO PROBLEMS ARE CONFRONTED,
NO SOLUTIONS SEARCHED FOR. EACH OF US NEEDS
TO WITHDRAW FROM THE CARES WHICH WILL
NOT WITHDRAW FROM US.

MAYA ANGELOU

THE PURSUIT, EVEN OF THE BEST THINGS,
OUGHT TO BE CALM AND TRANQUIL.

MARCUS TULLIUS CICERO

Happiness is your nature. It is not wrong
to desire it. What is wrong is seeking it
outside when it is inside.

Ramana Maharshi

ONLY THE DEVELOPMENT OF COMPASSION AND
UNDERSTANDING FOR OTHERS CAN BRING US THE
TRANQUILLITY AND HAPPINESS WE ALL SEEK.

DALAI LAMA

YOUR MIND WILL ANSWER MOST QUESTIONS IF YOU
LEARN TO RELAX AND WAIT FOR THE ANSWER.

WILLIAM S. BURROUGHS

LOOKING AT BEAUTY IN THE WORLD, IS THE
FIRST STEP OF PURIFYING THE MIND.

AMIT RAY

CREATIVITY IS ALLOWING YOURSELF TO MAKE
MISTAKES. ART IS KNOWING WHICH ONES TO KEEP.

SCOTT ADAMS

LET EVERYTHING HAPPEN TO YOU, BEAUTY AND
TERROR, JUST KEEP GOING, NO FEELING IS FINAL.

RAINER MARIA RILKE

SERENITY IS NOT FREEDOM FROM THE STORM,
BUT PEACE AMID THE STORM.

ANONYMOUS

THE MORE TRANQUIL A MAN BECOMES, THE GREATER IS HIS SUCCESS, HIS INFLUENCE, HIS POWER FOR GOOD. CALMNESS OF MIND IS ONE OF THE BEAUTIFUL JEWELS OF WISDOM.

JAMES ALLEN

REST AND REPOSE ARE AS MUCH A PART OF LIFE'S
JOURNEYS AS SEEING ALL WE CAME TO SEE.

GINA GREENLEE

PATIENCE IS THE CALM ACCEPTANCE THAT
THINGS CAN HAPPEN IN A DIFFERENT ORDER THAN
THE ONE YOU HAVE IN MIND.

DAVID G. ALLEN

Learn to calm down the winds of your mind,
and you will enjoy great inner peace.

Remez Sasson

This edition is published by Peony Press,
an imprint of Anness Publishing Ltd,
108 Great Russell Street, London WC1B 3NA
info@anness.com

www.annesspublishing.com; Twitter: @Anness_Books

Images courtesy of istock and canstock

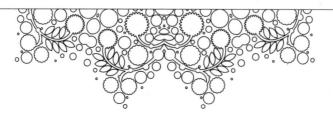